Be blessed end.

Tailored:
Being Fitted to
Perfection

Debbie Woods

HIGHERLIFE
PUBLISHING & MARKETING

Tailored: Being Fitted to Perfection

Published by
HigherLife Publishing & Marketing Inc.
PO Box 623307
Oviedo, FL 32762
www.ahigherlife.com

Scripture quotations, unless otherwise noted, are from the Revised Standard Version (RSV), 1952. Used by permission.

Paperback ISBN: 978-0-9989773-3-1
ebook ISBN: 978-0-9989773-4-8
Cover design: Bill Johnson
First Edition
17 18 19 20 21 22 — 9 8 7 6 5 4 3 2 1
Printed in the United States of America

Praise for Tailored

"Life is messy, and it often leaves one a bit torn and raggedy around the edges. Debbie Woods brings great hope and comfort to those of us who need to be 'mended.' Christ our Lord is the "master tailor," and He is always ready to pull us "out of the rag pile" and make us brand new—"tailored" by Him, in Him, and for Him! Debbie has done a wonderful work in His name for us all. To take time to read is to take time to be blessed."

Pastor Darien Bennet
The Trinity Church, Scottsdale, Arizona;
president, Men Coaching Men Discipleship Ministry;
president, Heart to Heat Christian Chaplaincy Program;
and author of *Your Next Step: J3 Discipleship Guide & Workbooks*

"*Tailored: Being Fitted to Perfection* is tender, winsome, authentic, and engaging and will point you straight to the grace of Jesus Christ. Satan tries to needle us with guilt and shame for our sin, but on these pages, Debbie has beautifully stitched the clear message of mending by the Master Tailor, who embraces us just the way we are with all our imperfections. The vulnerability of her own struggles, patched together with what she has learned in her everyday examples, will leave your heart impacted and encouraged with sound biblical truth, sage, and wit."

Shela-Lyn Boxberger
Author of *It's the Thought That Counts*;
National conference interpreter for Lifeway Christian Events

"I love *Tailored: Being Fitted to Perfection* even more than Debbie's first book, Mended, and I loved that one! I can identify so much with everything Debbie wrote, and I am sure so many will be encouraged because she validates their life struggles and spiritual journeys. The journey can be oh, so difficult, but it certainly helps to know that we are not alone in our struggles and that we are being "tailored" by The One Who loves us more than we can ever imagine."

Jan Dravecky
Executive Director, Endurance with Jan & Dave Dravecky;
co-author of *A Joy I'd Never Known: One Woman's Triumph Over Panic Attacks and Depression*

Dedication

I dedicate this book to Jesus, The Master Tailor. He graciously reclaimed me from life's rag pile, stitched me up, renewed me, and reused me. I have been damaged by life, but saved by grace and dressed in righteous robes. His never-ending mending has carried me from womb to white hair. Thank you, Jesus, my redeemer, restorer, rebuilder, rewarder.

Acknowledgments

I thank my husband, Tom, who also saved this raggedy girl more than forty-five years ago. Your continuing unconditional love and patience have healed my broken heart and bound up my wounds, just like Jesus.

Thank you to every Young Life leader, "Other Mother," Bible teacher, and "Soul Sister" who, at various times as needed, poured one vital drop or buckets of Living Water into me.

Special thanks to Denise Burnes and Jan Stephens, who believed in small clouds and cardinals as they prayed and supported me throughout this adventure.

Table of Contents

Part 2: "Little" Alterations

Preface

Tailored: refit, repinned, refined, revised, enhanced, transformed, custom-made, to adapt so as to make suitable for something specific.

Am I a late bloomer or just a slow learner? Jesus lifted me from the rag pile fifty years ago and began to mend the scraps of my soul. I was in desperate need to be freed from faults and defects, to be put in working order again. The Master Mender worked tenderly and endlessly to repair my shame, guilt, hopelessness. It was a big job. It continues to this day. I am still on the mend. Each day, Jesus gently resews my torn thoughts and patches my damaged attitude. How much longer can it take? Knowing that maturity is married to time, many more anniversaries with Jesus loom on the horizon!

God's Word gives me hope. Jesus said the poor in spirit (humble), those who mourn (repentant), and those who hunger and thirst for righteousness are blessed (see Matt. 5:1–6). I am aware of my remaining sinfulness, my tattered spirit, and I thirst for righteousness not yet attained. Jesus condemned the hypocrites for pretending to be what they were not. He also called out the Pharisees for their self-righteous, critical, judgmental spirits. But honesty and humility bring mending and blessedness. It is not a rapid process; the flesh does not give up easily. But as I am united with Christ, I am clothed in His perfect righteousness. I greatly rejoice, and my soul shall exult in my God (see Isa. 61:10). Amen.

What you see is what you get with me: the good, the bad, and the ugly. Lots of ugly. I can be a hypocrite, and I can be a Pharisee. My father taught me years ago that everyone is an idiot, and they are all aimed at me. I have been programmed from a young age to be critical, even harsh, when I observe the faulty behavior of others. Especially bad drivers. They are the worst. Jesus wants to reweave and renew my mind with humility, meekness, and mercy (see Matt. 5:3, 5, 7). Real mending and lasting change begin in my mind, in my thought patterns, which only God can transform to prove what is good and perfect (see Rom. 12:2).

Preface

Back to the Tailor! I am a regular there; I have a punch card with Jesus. My ingrained thoughts are frayed and stained. I come unraveled with worry, fear, insecurity, and anxiety. My seams split with impatience and irritability. Take off my old nature, Lord, and renew the spirit of my mind. Dress me in robes, created after Your likeness, in true righteousness and holiness (see Eph. 4:22–24). Fashion me to think on what is pure, lovely, and worthy of praise (see Phil. 4:8).

Jesus has given me His garment of life and hung me back on the hanger. When I fill my mind with His Word, rely on the Holy Spirit, confess, and repent quickly, I stay on that hanger. When I allow selfishness or Satan's lies to slash and slice into the fabric of my being, I slip off and land back in the rag pile. God continues to tailor and fashion me, as I can bear it, into a garment fitted perfectly to every good work (see 2 Tim. 3:17). Yes, I am still on the mend, but great is His faithfulness; His mercies are new every morning. The steadfast love of the Lord never ceases, and therefore I have hope (see Lam. 3:21–24). My message to you is that God can redesign and repurpose anyone at any time for their good and His glory.

These little thoughts have been gathered from my life, sermon notes, songs, and the inspired words of others jotted in my journals. At the time, I made no mention of authors and was not careful with quotations. As a result, I am unable to give credit where credit is due. Not every thought is original to me. However, "every good gift comes from above." Therefore, I will give my Holy "Ghost Writer" the glory.

Dear Reader

My unraveling began at a young age. Like you, perhaps, the small nips and slits grew larger over time. Slices and slashes by people and circumstances left me tattered in the rag pile. It was not pretty. I was forced to drop out of high school during a teenage pregnancy. Unspeakable pain. However, God, working unseen, salvaged the scraps of my life and allowed me to become an honored high school Spanish teacher, school board member, wife, and mother. He is The Master Tailor, indeed!

The mending has continued for a lifetime. Jesus repaired the biggest tears and blotted out the obvious stains first. The smaller snags and spots have taken longer. God whispers to me moment by moment. I have learned to be attentive to His regular speaking voice, His ordinary tone. "I will hear what

God, the Lord, will speak" (Ps. 85:8). In traffic, at the dentist's office, at the grocery store. Always. Everywhere. The nail salon becomes a cathedral and the car wash a chapel. The fabric of daily life is transformed to a seamless garment for the Lord. Jesus has gently patched me with His holy "cross" stitch through the Word and the Holy Spirit, adding a new hook and eye of purpose and joy.

> The fabric of daily life is transformed to a seamless garment for the Lord.

Be assured, the Master Tailor neither slumbers nor sleeps (see Ps. 121:4). His unceasing renewal is cosmetic surgery for the soul! Laugh with me. Bring your time-worn, stained, fragile, fraying heart, soul, and mind to Jesus, and be clothed in new raiment. No eye has seen, nor ear heard, nor the heart conceived what God has prepared for those who love Him (see 1 Cor. 2:9).

PART 1

Master Alterations

CHAPTER 1

This Beggar's Tin Cup
(Life Overflowing)

For the most part, mothers did not work outside the home when I was a child. My mother was an exception. She was not just a woman with five children, but also a teacher. While she carried professional obligations and responsibilities, there were no quick, easy conveniences to lighten the household duties. I never heard her complain; she just got it done. Busy from early morning until late at night, Mother did not have the time or energy needed to nurture and instruct us children. We were on our own. To me, our home seemed like a boarding house. We lived in the same residence and shared meals together. We followed the house rules. We were civil but independent, and we ate gallons of ice cream for comfort.

I was lost and empty. Alone. Fearful. Inadequate and unprepared. It has been stated that abandonment by one's mother is not fatal but causes a grievous, lifelong wound. While I could not articulate my unmet need, I felt it deeply. My soul was torn and ragged. Like a beggar, I picked up my tin cup and went out seeking alms and love from anyone I met.

> Like a beggar, I picked up my tin cup and went out seeking alms and love from anyone I met.

My cup was always outstretched. In desperation, I begged others to fill me. I was not enough. Not smart enough, pretty enough, athletic enough. Never loved enough, safe enough. Wouldn't someone assist this pitiful beggar? Proverbs 19:22 declares that we all crave loyalty and unfailing love. Aunt, uncle, teacher, girlfriend, boyfriend? Someone, anyone—please! Over time, a few dropped a coin or two into my cup. Occasionally, I received paper money from a generous soul. Frequently, the offering was counterfeit, metal slugs, or foreign coins—useless. The donor faked the appearance of generosity just for show, leaving me mocked and still empty.

Though my father and my mother forsake me, the Lord will take me up (see Prov. 27:10). Jesus took me up and began to mend my tattered life through a Young Life ministry. I learned the story and the song of the woman at the well who was seeking things that could not satisfy. Then she heard Jesus say, "Draw from my well that never shall run dry." Slowly, I learned that Jesus provides Living Water (see John 4:13–15). The Samaritan woman's only humble,

> ## Jesus took me up and began to mend my tattered life through a Young Life ministry.

grateful response, and mine, could be, "Fill my cup, Lord. I lift it up, Lord. Quench this thirsting of my soul!"

O, taste and see that the Lord is good! Take just a sip. Jesus did not ask me to chug his Word or to swallow the whole thing at once. New in faith, I held on to my cup but began to search the Word of God for everlasting life. I found Jesus with open arms for those poor in spirit, those who hunger and thirst for righteousness. I got in line! "Come and drink," he called. In time, I learned that as I accepted His grace and began an abiding relationship with Jesus, He would lead me beside still waters, and my cup would overflow (see Psalm 23).

> **This beggar had found the Water of Life.**

This beggar had found the Water of Life. I had to tell my other beggar friends the Good News so they could come to the banquet prepared for them.

My mother grew up during the Depression. She explained that shabby-looking hobos came through the neighborhoods looking for food or perhaps a clean shirt or warm coat. When they found the home of a generous soul, they marked the street out front with a giant X so other ratty hobos could find help, too. Such a perfect metaphor for sharing the Gospel. Come, friend; bring your empty cup. I know where to find water! Remove your stained rags and be redressed in new cloth as white as snow (see Isa. 1:18). "With joy, you will draw water from the wells of salvation. And you will say in that day: 'Give thanks to the Lord, call upon His name; make known His deeds among the nations, proclaim that His name is exalted'" (Isa. 12:3–4).

When I drink from the well of the Word, I am refreshed and quenched. Foolishly, I wander off with my cup again, to see if there is more somewhere else. Raw cookie dough, ice cream, shopping, vacations? Wrong! I always end up parched and dry, lifeless. God's Word promises

> When I drink from the well of the Word, I am refreshed and quenched.

that those who believe in Christ will never thirst. God pours out His Spirit on the thirsty and floods their dry grounds. He satisfies the soul in drought, making it a garden. His waters never fail. When the poor and needy seek water, the Lord will answer them. He will open rivers and fountains, making the wilderness a pool that men may see and know that the hand of God has done it (see John 4 and Isaiah 41, 44, 58). Often, when I realize I am threadbare in spots and naked again, I attempt my own mending. It never holds. This beggar returns to the Tailor, and He always receives me again.

Forsaken by parents and "looking for love in all the wrong places," I was taken up by Jesus. I meditate on what He has done. I stretch out my hands to Him; my soul thirsts for Him like a parched land. Each morning, I hear word of His steadfast, unfailing love, and I am renewed (see Ps. 143:5–8 and Lam. 3:22–23). I am enough. I am loved. My cup overflows. I wear the garment of salvation and the robes of righteousness (Isa. 1:11).

Today I will empty my cup of things that leave me thirsting and exchange them for the grace and satisfaction only God's Living Water can provide. I will delight in my coat of many colors woven just for me by my Father who loves me.

CHAPTER 2

Getting Dressed (Opportunity)

My mother loved clothes. I didn't know it at the time, but she was the first "clothes horse" in my life. I believe part of her motivation to work as a teacher was to supplement not only our family income but also her wardrobe budget. Most women in education are not known for their fashionable attire, but Mother was. And not just higher-quality traditional clothes, but high-style, funky stuff. In the 1960s, she added psychedelic flair with hot pink and paisley tights. I didn't care. I barely noticed. But my younger brother was mortified. He wanted her to be a Plain Jane mom and drab teacher—nothing flashy or attention-getting. Never happened. She is still stylin' at age ninety-five, the fashion icon of her nursing home!

Our relationship was threadbare. Oddly, although she was an elementary school teacher, she did not nurture or instruct her own children. We were on our own. Our hearts and souls were hanging by a thread.

Our relationship was threadbare.

Once, after receiving a compliment about how well she had raised me, she candidly replied, "Well, thank you, but I can't take credit. She pretty much raised herself." I was stunned by her unembarrassed admission—and felt validated. Thankfully, early in my youth, God provided "other mothers" to stitch me up. Their gentle patching held me together.

I was expelled from high school on a Friday. By late Sunday night, out of time, I had to tell my parents. I was six months pregnant and could not return to school on Monday. Miserable.

Terrible. Horrible. Regrettably, it was Mother's birthday. Surprise! The last thread of our relationship was clipped.

Three months later, it got even worse. Unimaginably worse. Unbearably worse. I gave birth to my parents' first grandchild and gave her up for adoption on their twenty-fifth wedding anniversary. Really. God's timing seemed so cruel, so unnecessary. He is the Ruler of the Universe, the Keeper of Time, yet He allowed these special occasions to be spoiled by tears and tragedy. Or did He have a greater plan?

> Our worldly wardrobe is not enough.

"Behold, I stand at the door and knock; if anyone hears my voice and opens the door, I will come in and eat with him, and he with me" (Rev. 3:20). Jesus was knocking on my mother's heart, offering fellowship and salvation. He was graciously asking to mend her life and reweave her family relationships. My pregnancy was a loud knocking; notice was being given. "Open the door to Me!" On her birthday and anniversary, the pounding was even louder. This was opportunity calling! A heart-changing, life-changing opportunity. If today you hear His voice, harden not your heart (see Heb. 3:15).

Our worldly wardrobe is not enough. Life can strip us bare. People rip and tear at the very fabric of our souls. Circumstances slice and shred us into a tattered pile of rags. We continually try to cover the outside with style, with what is in vogue, only to look ridiculous in photos years later. 1970s, anyone? Oh, my! But inside, we become zombies, the ratty walking dead. Only Jesus can bring us back to life, to wholeness. He clothes us with the garments of salvation and covers us with the robe of righteousness (see Isa. 61:10). Only Jesus can salvage us from the rag basket to freedom and purpose, redressing us by hand for His Master Designer Collection. Unique, one-of-a kind, original, priceless creations. Yay!

Mother had moved so far into her clothes closet and away from God that she didn't see her need for the Master Tailor. She had no desire for His Presence and refused to be open to His fellowship. The Lord's loud knocking, His attempt to rekindle an awareness of her need, was ignored. He brought a birthday gift and an anniversary gift with His nail-scarred hands but was turned away. That was the real tragedy of that situation. 'Take care, lest there be in any of you an evil, unbelieving heart, leading you to fall away from the living God. But exhort one another every day, as long as it is called 'today,' that none of you may be hardened by the deceitfulness of sin" (Heb. 3:12). "Sin" simply means leaving God out. It is an attitude of the heart that leads to our actions—sin. My mother left God out.

Years later, I invited her to the women's Bible study I attended. We also took her to church with our family each week. She heard God's Living Word on a regular basis. As Jesus describes in Matthew 13, the parable of the sower, the good seed of Scripture, has been cast on the soil of my mother's heart. I cannot say whether it was eaten by birds, choked out by thorns, scorched, and withered by the sun, or took root. Only God knows. At age ninety-five, there is yet time for a harvest. I can only pray and watch.

Today, if Jesus knocks, I will not harden my heart, but rather run quickly to open the door. I will welcome His presence, His fellowship, and any gifts He might bring.

CHAPTER 3

Peace and Laughter (Purpose)

My father wanted nothing more than peace and quiet. In a home with five children, his desires were thwarted daily. Add to that a long commute to a job he hated, and life was bleak. His mantra was, "I have to pay for five college tuitions and four weddings," so he pressed on. "The Greatest Generation" knew the meaning of duty, for sure.

Dad was a highly intelligent man. He had attended law school after his four-year service in World War II but had to quit before graduating to support his new family, his little "baby boomers." His sharp wit and broad humor helped grease the tracks of life, keeping him in line and moving forward. He was a man of few words, and when he spoke, it was generally in fun or in anger. We knew to tread lightly. Each of us kids inherited

> I became the hypervigilant keeper of family happiness.

his humor, which served us well throughout our lives, along with a profound sense of duty.

And I learned to beware of anger.

As a middle child with no distinguishable gifts or talents, I found myself in the role of peacemaker and entertainer. I was not the brilliant first-born, the boy-child, or the adorable, last-born little girls, so I became the hypervigilant keeper of family happiness. In times of tension, I intervened to calm disputes among the siblings. When I was involved, I gave in and gave up avoiding an eruption. Don't get Dad mad. Peace at any cost. When life was bland, I teased and cajoled. If someone didn't have milk coming out his or her nose at the dinner table, I was a failure!

As Dad paid for yet another wedding, I could see I was needed. Humor is not the only trait we siblings share. We tend to be perfectionists, and we like to be in control. The Bride had a plan and a schedule, but I wasn't sensing any joy. So, I, The Entertainer, had my own plan. At the wedding rehearsal, we all did as we were told. But as the sisters/bridesmaids strolled down the aisle and gathered at the altar, I gave each of them a pair of "nose glasses" with big, black, bushy eyebrows and mustaches to wear. We had our backs to my father and The Bride as they neared the altar. On cue, we turned in unison to shock and amuse the crowd. Success! The tension was broken.

If only milk had come from their noses, my joy would have been complete. I should invent something...

Nose glasses became the family standard. We wear them on special occasions. We wear them on the back of our heads facing the camera backwards in group pictures. We have rubber stamps of a nose to adorn notes and letters, nose stationery, and nose greeting cards and e-mail images. In honor of Dad, we all wore nose glasses at his memorial service. Even the grandkids—too cute! We sent him off for eternity with a laugh.

Being a peacemaker and entertainer became my coping mechanism, but it was not healthy. I drew no personal boundaries for my emotional safety. I went along, gave in, said yes when I should have said no, or held my tongue to keep the peace and please everyone else. I used humor to defray tension and unpleasant situations. I became self-deprecating to the point of insecurity. I took the brunt of any storm to protect others from harm. My humor became cynical and sarcastic. Not good. I needed to mend my ways.

> Peacemaking is a godly virtue to be sought.

I found truth, as always, in God's Word. "Blessed are the peacemakers, for they shall be called sons of God" (Matt. 5:9). In the Sermon on the Mount, Jesus tells us the qualities He wants to develop in us. Peacemaking is a godly virtue to be sought. God designs us to be relational, both with Him and with others. "Behold, how good and pleasant it is when brothers dwell in unity (peace)" (Ps. 133:1). While raising my three sons, that became a family verse. It was even on a magnet on our refrigerator! Amen? "Peace I leave with you; my peace I give to you; not as the world gives do I give to you. Let not your heart be troubled, neither let it be dismayed" (John 14:27). I had to gain wisdom, discernment, timing, truth, and courage and learn God's purpose. Only He can truly bring peace, renewal, and restoration to torn and fraying relationships.

"Blessed are the humorous, for they bring a gift from God." Well, that isn't in the Sermon on the Mount, but it should

God will fill your mouth with laughter.

be, right? God's Word is full of statements concerning laughter and joy. Make a joyful noise unto the Lord! In Thy presence is the fullness of joy. Let those who love Your name be joyful in You (see Ps. 66, 16, 5). There is a time to weep and a time to laugh. Weeping may tarry the night, but joy comes in the morning. You, Lord, have turned my wailing and mourning to dancing and have clothed me with a garment of joy (see Eccles. 3:4, Psalm 30). God will fill your mouth with laughter.

When we were restored, our mouths were filled with laughter and our tongues with shouts of joy (see Job 8, Psalm 126).

Best of all, Psalm 2 tells us that He who sits in heaven laughs. How great is that? God has a sense of humor, and He designed us to laugh. Love that! It has been said that laughter is a tension dissolver, pain reliever, antidote to anxiety, and life's shock absorber. I gain perspective as I laugh at myself and with God, picturing one of my numerous calamities as a scene with Lucy and Ethel or from Friends. Laughter is the best medicine.

As God repairs my damaged approach to life, His purpose for peacemaking and laughter become blessings, gifts, rather than my default setting. By the grace of the Holy Spirit, I am clothed in a new garment with gladness of heart, not the armor of self-protection.

I still find myself in the role of peacemaker within my small circle of influence, and God is glorified when "brothers and sisters live in unity." And laughter is my daily sword against melancholy, depression, and the Enemy who comes to steal, kill, and destroy (see John 10). I still intend to laugh until it hurts, until I cry, until I wet my pants. That is the sign of a great day! May I offer you a glass of milk? Blessed be the Lord, who sits in heaven and laughs!

Today I will strive to bring peace where and when I can, and I will rest in the peace of the Lord, which passes understanding. Although there is a time to weep, I will find joy in the Lord today by the grace of the Holy Spirit.

CHAPTER 4

From Duty to Beauty (Service)

I was born into duty. I had no choice. No questions asked. My family heritage is British. Stiff upper lip. Keep calm and carry on. Never mind your happiness; do your duty. To give up a duty is a grave dereliction. It was not spoken; it was assumed. And modeled every day.

My parents were part of the Greatest Generation. They survived the Great Depression and sacrificed their personal lives and plans for four years during World War II. They continued their duty without complaint as they raised their family. My father endured a lengthy, unpleasant commute to a job he disliked for almost thirty years. Mother raised five children while teaching first grade full time, with none of the conveniences moms have today. Chores were done manually, food prepared from scratch. Head down; press on. Lives of quiet desperation, with no joy.

As a child, I knew to do my duty without supervision. Bed made, teeth brushed, homework completed. Routine without question, as natural as breathing. Moral expectations and ethical responsibilities were innate. Be good, be polite, be honest, be kind, be punctual, be quiet.

Naturally, I carried this preprogrammed thinking into my adult life. Duty became my middle name. As a wife and mother of three sons, I was always steady, dependable, trustworthy, responsible. Always. I didn't really have a life, but I certainly had a schedule. I did my duty for the benefit of others, finding some satisfaction, but not great pleasure. After years of menial labor and mundane chores, I was frayed and unraveling.

Finally, I woke up. One day, while terribly sick and weak, I found myself pushing a basket of dirty clothes down the hall to the laundry room on my hands and knees. Duty called! Wait. What is wrong with this picture? This cannot be the abundant life Jesus promises, a life of joy and purpose. I had become Martha, serving without delight (see Luke 10). Jesus was reminding me, like He did Martha, that only "one thing" is important: serving the Kingdom with eyes on Jesus and a heart set on Him. The Master Tailor started stitching and reweaving my attitude.

I had become Martha, serving without delight

OK, I liked that idea, but my reality was still full of responsibilities: groceries to buy, patios to sweep, a driveway to hose off, dusting to do, more groceries, vacuuming, unending sweaty socks and jocks to wash. And in my four-man household, toilets to clean! Just sayin'. Did I mention the groceries? Trivial duties, uneventful routine, with nothing to show for the effort. Do it all again tomorrow. Happily, I learned the deeper meaning of menial and mundane. The Latin root implies "dwelling or household," connections, family, household ties. This understanding helped me see that I was, like Martha, working, preparing, serving for the benefit and pleasure of others, my family. Duty was redefined for me as humility, perseverance, and sacrifice. Godly character. OK, but something was still missing. God was not done with His patching just yet.

How do I get from drudgery and duty to beauty?

How do I get from drudgery and duty to beauty? How is perfunctory daily life transformed to gentle service of faithfulness? Spiritual eyes are needed to discern the ordinary fabric of life as woven with loving attention, as a seamless garment for the Lord. Do not despise the small things; God is in them (see Zech. 4:10). "Duty" and "beauty" are not just poetic rhymes. They have a fundamental relationship. If I examine duty closer, and in The Light, I find beauty in the details of God's great, eternal purpose.

As I look at duty from a new angle, from God's heavenly perspective. I find enthusiasm for the commonplace. Duty becomes glorified in the celestial light. Spiritual eyes bring a clear vision that every minute of life's structure is a glorious detail of the completed whole that God has designed. When

I work "unto the Lord, not unto men" (see Col. 3:23, Eph. 6:7), dry, common-life duties become stair steps to heaven, spiritual advancement. As I serve, the smallest things unite me with Him. I will dust, vacuum, weed, wash windows, scrub showers, scrape gum off shoes, wipe up spills, clean up vomit, and empty trash without whining or complaint, as a love offering to God. Most of the time...

Duty becomes glorified in the celestial light.

I want the mind of Christ, who gave up equality with God and humbled Himself to become a bondservant (see Phil. 2:5–8). I look upward for an awakening of my soul to lift the monotonous tasks and dull routine to the higher purposes of God. Details are boring and tiresome, but they cause little daily submissions of my will. My selfishness, unhappiness, and distressed spirit disappear when I accept my holy service. I seek after cheerfulness to trample out discontent and break off murmuring (see Phil. 2:4, Num. 11:1). "I delight to do God's will" (Ps. 40:8) is easier to say in the bigger issues of life, and at times, with a self-righteous undertone. I need to remember, "This is what God is asking me to do today, this minute (repeatedly)" to find joy, privilege, and beauty in duty. I will walk with integrity of heart (wholeness, trustworthiness) within my house (see Psalm 101).

Today I humbly bow my knee to cheerfully serve anyone in any way that God asks of me. I will redeem every chore, turning it into prayer. I will sew my part of the seamless garment for the Lord.

CHAPTER 5

Brave Irene (Grace)

I once heard the story of Brave Irene, the young daughter of a seamstress. Her mother had just finished a beautiful dress for the duchess but became sick and was unable to deliver it. It was up to little Irene to take the gown in its huge box to the palace. Uphill, through wind and snow, she trudged. The wind grew fierce, and darkness came. Irene could not tell if she was even on the right path, but she refused to give up. She fell and twisted her ankle but dragged on. Her teeth chattered. Ultimately, all ended well.

Such a great story to share with my children. Perseverance. Commitment. Determination. Duty. Helpfulness. Self-sacrifice. Push on. Remember Brave Irene. You can do it.

I remember many Brave Irene assignments.

Then I applied it to myself. Others will laugh, but it can get very cold in the desert during the winter. Really. I'm talking 50 degrees! (Remember, my summers are 115 degrees and higher.) My daily early-morning walk can become quite a challenge. I wear a jacket, gloves, scarf, and hat, but the wind still gets to me. And my course is uphill! (Both ways, as my father used to say. Wink, wink!) I channel Brave Irene. I press on. My nose runs when I'm cold. I sniff. Sniff again. Stop for a tissue to blow. I am undaunted.

As I reflect on life, I remember many Brave Irene assignments. God would hand me a big box and say, "Go." But I was unprepared and frightened, and the path was difficult. It will get dark, and I will lose my way.

Carry yourself through childhood unprotected and unguided. I can't. Carry this baby for nine months and give her up, unseen. I can't. Carry yourself to the desert and sit alone for ten years. I can't. Carry your father through his final months, until death. I can't.

So many other big boxes over a lifetime. How did I ever make it to the palace for a happy ending? Only by the grace of God. Not by intelligence, or talent, or character, or experience, or training. Sometimes I even refused. "I will not! You cannot make me."

"But, daughter, this is important. You must go."

"Fear not...I have called you by name. When you pass through the waters I will be with you; and through rivers, they shall not overwhelm you; when you walk through fire you shall not be burned...For I am the Lord your God...Your Savior" (Isa. 43:1–3). Brave Irene was truly alone, but I have Jesus to guide and sustain me. He does not faint or grow weary. He gives power to the faint, and to those who have no might, He increases strength. He promises to help me and uphold me with His victorious right hand (see Isaiah 40 and 41). I can press on, assured of His presence.

I do not always want to be a servant, a box deliverer, for the Lord. I want to stay home by a cozy fire. I see the snow and hear the wolves howling outside. And it is windy. I hate the wind. My nose runs. Yet I hear God say, "Behold my servant, whom I uphold, my chosen, in whom my soul delights. I have put my spirit in (her)...(She) will not fail or be discouraged" (see Isa. 42:1–4). The psalm goes on to instruct me in the ways of a servant: act in the power of the Holy Spirit, be humble and gentle, show perseverance, be a light to others, walk by faith, and remember who's the boss!

> My Father is the Master Tailor.

I do not yet know what other big boxes God has prepared for me to carry. I want to live like the Proverbs 31 woman, who is not afraid of snow, taking each box from the hand of God with strength and dignity, laughing at the times to come without fear. Will my next box contain cancer? Alzheimer's? My husband's unexpected, early death? A tragedy involving a grandchild? Chronic pain? What might rip the fabric of my soul, my life as I want it? I smile when I remember that Brave Irene's mother was a seamstress. My Father is the Master Tailor. He will continue to patch and reinforce me for a lifetime. And I will make it to His palace and attend the ball. Amen.

Today I will face whatever comes, confident that the Lord knows my path, guides me, and sustains me each step of the way. Whatever box He assigns me is important.

CHAPTER 6

October Light (Cleansing)

need order. I love order. I crave order. I make my bed before I leave the room when I wake up so it will be orderly when I re-enter the room. No rumpled bedding or pillows strewn about. When my bed looks chaotic, my brain is chaotic. Order is peace. Order is calm. Order is the way God designed the world, not in chaos, for our well-being (see Isa. 48:18 and 1 Cor. 14:33). Systematic, regulated, methodized. Heaven on earth.

In a home with three boys, order takes effort. Herculean effort. Nevertheless, I arose each day undaunted. A place for everything, and everything in its place. I was swimming upstream against a tide of clothing, toys, sports equipment, backpacks, school projects, and paperwork, but I became an Olympian. Beds were made; bath towels rehung; toothpaste wiped from the sink; mirrors cleaned; shoes corralled; all dishes placed in the dishwasher (never the counter or the sink!); and mail, magazines, and newspapers neatly sorted and stored away. Always. I circled endlessly, like a shark with black, unblinking eyes, organizing and keeping everything contained, tidy.

> In a home with three boys, order takes effort.

Friends often commented that my house was always "clean." Not true, I was quick to confess. It looked clean because it was neat, but I was not overzealous about cleaning. I did enjoy cleaning, but I was not one to use a Q-tip and bleach in the nooks and crannies. Ceiling fans and floorboards were not a priority. Sofas and curtains did not get vacuumed regularly. No, cleanliness is not next to godliness; order is next to godliness. I was the Goddess of Order.

The autumn light of October shook my world. I had a large window by the tub in my master bathroom. As seasons changed, so did the lighting. I cleaned the sinks, mirrors, and countertops daily and Swiffer-ed the floor two to three times a week. (Toilets, tubs, and showers on the weekend, along with a wet mop on the floor.) I neatly rolled extra towels and piled them in a spa-like pyramid. Lovely. Peaceful. Orderly. But this new October light revealed a horror! Little hairs and tiny, unseen dust bunnies covered the floor. How could this be? We do not have a dog. Where did this come from? I am not a clean freak, but this was unacceptable. Easy solution: I would dry-mop daily.

> I was the Goddess of Order.

Light exposes the hidden, the unseen. I was content until the truth was revealed to me. And so it is in the spiritual realm. Jesus is the light of the world (see John 8:12). We are satisfied with our own goodness until we see Him face to face. What is done in the darkness is revealed in the light. There is no place for evil-doers to hide (see Psalm 34 and 139). All our goodness is seen to be filthy rags (see Isaiah 64).

Although Jesus enlightened and cleansed me in my youth, He sheds new light in every season of life. Throughout young adulthood, married life, and motherhood, Jesus was a lamp unto my feet, leading the way (see Psalm 119). His light disclosed rips in my heart, frays in my thinking, and a damaged attitude. He gently repaired my insecurities, selfishness, and fears, making me sound again. In middle age, retirement, and beyond, the Master Tailor continues to stand me before His mirror and shed the light of His Word on me, revealing my previously unseen flaws and threadbare self. He tenderly uncovers the hidden things, the secret places (see Daniel 2 and Jeremiah 23). Little hairs of pride and dust bunnies of bitterness are laid bare to Him, to whom we must give an account (see Hebrews 4). Where did these come from? Can I blame the dog? I need to mop daily. Jesus lovingly and carefully refashions me and perfectly fits me for His purpose. I am clothed in a new garment—not randomly assembled, but tailor-made uniquely for me.

When the Light of the World enlightens my understanding, I leave behind my blind heart to walk in truth. I put off my former, corrupt, stained conduct (envy, jealousy, irritability, defensiveness, impatience, laziness, judgment, critical spirit) and put on my new self, in righteousness and holiness. I come out of darkness and walk as a child of the light. I have no place for unfruitful works of darkness, but rather the fruit of the Spirit in all goodness and truth. (see Ephesians 4 and 5).

I press on in my fight for order. Throw out gossip, scrub out harsh judgments, flush out pride, freshen up with a vase of mercy and compassion. I want all the towels of life rolled and stacked into a pyramid, but I have learned that the battle is never won. Just when I think I'm all tidy and cleaned up, Jesus brings the light of a new season to uncover the truth, keeping me humble and in need of grace. I am still on the mend.

Today I will willingly and humbly look directly into the light of God's Word to see what it may reveal within me. I will confess and repent, asking for grace to clean up any mess or stain previously unseen.

CHAPTER 7

Confession (Impatience)

After running several errands in the Arizona summer heat before lunch, I was hot, hungry, and ready to go home. But instead, I pushed my luck by going to Kohl's department store. I would just run in, grab one item, pay cash, and get out, completing my "to do" list, right? Noooo!

I started with a clerk who sent me to the wrong department, in the wrong direction, and ended twenty hungry, frustrated minutes later with the same clerk, who could not remove the antitheft device or scan the price correctly without calling for assistance. I was fried. My fake smile and pretend patience were obvious. Then I remembered: I had just left the Family Christian store and was still carrying the bag with its name and logo for all to see. Oh, the painful conviction and shame. I am just pitiful and should not be allowed in public. I had to laugh and thank her for her efforts, trying to ease the tension, but I feared the damage was done. The name of Christ was disgraced.

Another time, it was Senior Day at the grocery store. I knew better than to attempt shopping on Senior Day, but I, too, am a senior and entitled to a few perks now and then. I went. Determined to be patient and gracious, I endured little old couples walking slowly no, aimlessly. They had forgotten where they were. They had forgotten what they were shopping for. They had forgotten that they were not the only ones shopping that day. This was their highlight adventure of the month, and they were in no hurry to return home.

As patience ebbed, I was blocked from one aisle by a couple and their cart. I waited. And waited. They remained oblivious to my presence. I cleared my throat. No good. I softly and gently said to the gentleman, "Excuse me. Can I get by you, please?"

His brazen, snide, response? "Well, I don't know if you can or not, but you may!"

A grammar lesson—really? Do I ram him with my cart (accidentally) and then call for "cleanup on aisle six"? Help me, Jesus.

I passed them, but it was not over. My head spun, and my black, evil heart vomited up thoughts:

- "I didn't come here for a grammar lesson, old man."
- "So sorry to offend you, O Lord High Grammarian!"
- "Hey, move it or park it!"
- "If I need a grammar lesson, you need an etiquette lesson!"

Lovely thoughts; so Christ-like. No kindness, gentleness, or self-control from the fruit of the Holy Spirit in my grocery cart that day (see Gal. 5:22).

Jesus was waiting for me at the other end of aisle six. I was ashamed to face Him. He sent me home for a "Time Out." I had reacted like a rude child—like a brat, really. I was also being a bitch, a grown self-entitled woman—combined, I was a "brach." At home, I wrote "BRACH" on my dunce cap and sat in the corner. I really should not be allowed in public. And I should never wear a cross necklace.

> # Jesus was waiting for me at the other end of aisle six.

Impatience: a strong annoyance; displeasure at the unintentional faults and failures of others. It is a heart condition insisting that others conform to my expectations. Selfish, superior, self-righteous. Such an ungodly attitude. Controlling. An ugly stain on the fabric of my soul.

In my flesh, patience is not my automatic, go-to response. Never. Who do I think I am? My faults and flaws irritate others daily, too. But I have reasons, excuses, justifications for my failures. Certainly, my offense can be overlooked, right? Grace, please. I'm trying. I didn't mean to do that. Oops!

God's patience and grace abound to me. If not, as one Bible teacher often said, He would just reach down and pinch my head off. Ha! I need to be rinsed out and rewoven, with the blotch of impatience washed out and redressed in love. Love is patient; love is kind (see 1 Cor. 13). Paul urges us to "put on," clothe ourselves, in patience (see Col. 3:12). Only Jesus, through His Holy Spirit, can make that alteration in me.

> God sews these virtues into the garment of my life repeatedly.

The fruit of His Spirit is love, patience, gentleness, kindness, and self-control (see Gal. 5:22–23). God sews these virtues into the garment of my life repeatedly. I am a regular at His tailor shop, a frequent customer of His, repeatedly needing His holy "cross" stitches.

Today I will set aside my selfish expectations, my annoyance with the faults and failures of others, and put on grace-colored

glasses to view others with patience and gentleness—as Jesus sees me.

CHAPTER 8

Spanish Instagram (Unending Mending)

I know a picture is worth a thousand words. Therefore, a video is worth ten thousand. When I check in with family and friends on Instagram, I find a variety of photos, from breathtaking to hilarious. If the post is a video, I learn so much more. The details found in the before and after offer a bigger picture and a better shared experience.

Spanish grammar lesson: The past is discussed in Spanish with a different understanding than English. Briefly, a single incident becomes a snapshot, using preterit—an adjective that expresses a past action or state. An action that is repeated or ongoing is spoken of as a video, using the imperfect tense—used, in Spanish, to refer to actions that have happened in the past repeatedly. I love that nuance. It can be difficult for English speakers to learn, but it is critical to explaining past actions.

> Jesus used her kindness to mend my damaged selfies.

The video of my life is "imperfect." Individual photos of my history can be breathtaking or hilarious, like Instagram, but they can also be tragic. There is a vast variety of snapshots in my memory, but I choose not to focus on any single one. My video recording tells a different, more comprehensive story.

A wise, loving friend first brought this to my attention while we were in college. Literally, I had taken all the photos of my high school years and torn them in pieces. Having been a pregnant teenager kicked out of school, I expressed to her that those years were a worthless disaster. She graciously disagreed. I was reminded that during that time I had formed many significant friendships, achieved academic success, and attained athletic recognition before "it just ended poorly." Jesus used her kindness to mend my damaged selfies. Rather than a scrapbook of individual pictures, I revisited my personal video to see the broader, ongoing "imperfect" story of my life. With my Spanish education minor to reinforce this insight, a different approach to evaluating the past emerged.

It is not just my high school years that have some ugly pictures. Some PMS-day photos reveal a wacky woman on the verge of lunacy. The traffic cameras on my driving route capture a crazed, impatient woman. Surveillance cameras at the grocery store show me, bug-eyed behind a slow, chatty person at checkout who forgot to present her coupons and now can't find her credit card. I look repulsive. Delete, delete, delete. Not proud moments, but not the entire story, either.

A single snapshot of Mary Magdalene before her encounter with Christ would show a struggling, tattered, deeply afflicted woman possessed by seven demons (see Luke 8:2). I imagine her dirty, disheveled, and tortured. The individual snapshot tells me she is without hope and discarded, avoided by others. But, oh, the glorious triumph of her life video! After her liberation, her mending and restoration by Jesus, Mary becomes one of the most beautiful characters of the Bible. She is mentioned fourteen times in the Gospel, which is more than most of the apostles. Like the repeated, habitual actions of the Spanish imperfect, she kept showing up, over and over. She owed much and therefore gave much—not on occasion, but daily. Mary Magdalene was transformed, restored, and renewed by the Master Tailor. She was the final follower at the cross and the first at the grave. Jesus blessed her faithfulness by allowing her to be the first at the resurrection and the first commissioned to proclaim the Good News to the brethren.

> Jesus commissions me to redress and renew other raggedy souls.

What a precious, personal scene when Jesus speaks to Mary outside the tomb (see John 20:11–18). As she wept, He said to her "Mary," and she was immediately comforted. Throughout my life video, Jesus has wiped my tears, patched, and rewoven my rags, and comforted me in unique and personal ways. With each encounter, through His Word or in prayer, I find hope, freedom, and purpose, just like Mary Magdalene. Jesus commissions me to redress and renew other raggedy souls. I, like Mary, can joyfully shout, "I have been with Jesus, and He has called me by name!" I want to love much and serve much. I will keep showing up until the last day. *Gracias a Dios.*

Today I will accept my imperfect self, my imperfect life, and keep showing up to be patched, tailored, and loved by Jesus as He calls me by name.

CHAPTER 9

Main Character (My Bit Part)

High school students fret and stress about the small stuff daily. It is big stuff to them, and when I was a teacher, they frequently brought it to my Spanish class. Zits, bad-hair days, parents, besties, ex-besties, choir tryouts, play rehearsals, football practices, volleyball tournaments, Homecomings, final exams, report cards, prom dates, prom dresses—big stuff. Time to put my lesson plan on hold and teach a life lesson.

One day, I drew a fifteen-foot blue line with arrows at each end across two whiteboards. The line represented eternity, infinity. I added a small red dot to represent the year. I asked the students to imagine their lives, in the context of the world's population, within the red dot. I asked each student to pinpoint the current day within his or her entire life. This exercise enables us to gain perspective. Will this issue matter in a week, month, year, ten years, to anyone but you? Of course, some of them will, but for a moment, consider how God sees the eternal spectrum.

Consider how God sees the eternal spectrum.

I do this, too. People and circumstances disrupt my goal of smooth sailing and easy days. Broken ankle, broken microwave, sick children, dead car battery, Christmas coming, taxes due, crazy neighbor—big stuff, right? Life can be overwhelming. Dana Perino is the former Bush White House press secretary. Her high-profile job and the constant pressure she faced are unimaginable to me. She has explained that she handled it by realizing that most of us are not that important. What? Where does that leave me? God sits above the circle of the Earth, and its inhabitants are like grasshoppers (see Isa. 49:22). Now, that gives me a higher point of view! When I look from God's field of vision, my petty irritations, annoyances, and fretful worries diminish.

I have learned that every life is a drama with heroes and villains, but the main character is always Jesus. Not me. I am just an "extra," and I play a bit part. The pressure is off! The spotlight is not on me. Phew. On this eternal world stage, God is the author, producer, choreographer, and director of everything. Jesus is His star. The Holy Spirit gets into the act by prompting me what to say (see Luke 12:12).

> **The main character is always Jesus.**

Shakespeare recognized that all the world is a stage, and all the men and women are merely players. We have our entrances and our exits, playing many parts in our time (see As You Like It, act 2, scene 7). My roles have been daughter, sister, friend, student, teacher, wife, mother, aunt, grandmother, and more. Shakespeare paints a dark picture when he says, "I am but a walking shadow that struts and frets my hour on the stage and then is seen no more (see Macbeth, act 5, scene 5). I want a happier ending.

Gratefully, God is the author and producer of my life, and I will see the goodness of the Lord in the land of the living. I don't have to wait for heaven, for eternity. He is sovereign over every detail. He does what pleases Him (see Ps. 115:3 and 135:6). He is full of pity and compassion for his "grasshoppers." He is pleased to help the righteous, those who love Him (see 2 Chron. 16:9). Take that, Shakespeare!

> God is the author and producer of my life.

It has been said that, compared to eternity in our heavenly mansion, this life is just one night in an inconvenient hotel. Not enough towels, pillow too flat, ice machine broken, noisy neighbor. I will handle these vexations with patience and perspective, with grace and humor.

For everything, there is a season. Like my teenage students, I have times to weep and mourn and suffer loss, but it is all under the hand of my living God. I will be still and know that He is God (see Ps. 46:10). I will cease striving and acknowledge His supremacy. Everything unfolds at God's appointed time. None of His plans for me can be thwarted; His purposes for me will be established (see Job 42:2 and Prov. 19:21). He's got this. He has my back! "The Lord preserves the simple; he saved me!' (Ps. 116:6) His love, mercy, and faithfulness are renewed every morning.

Today I will trust the Author and Producer of my life, who wisely sets the stage and directs the players. I will keep my eyes on the main character, Jesus, follow His lead, and wait for the Holy Spirit to prompt me.

CHAPTER 10

Jesus Is My Fitbit
(An Intentional Heart)

Within the month, two friends showed me their Fitbits. A Fitbit is an exercise and health monitor of sorts. They were excited to explain how the little wireless wristband tracked their steps, distance, calories burned, water consumed, and other bits of information. "Interesting," I thought, "but I'm quite active and not at all techie, so this is not for me."

Wrong. The Holy Spirit kept nudging me (nagging me) until I purchased one for myself. If today you hear His voice, harden not your heart, right? OK, let's do this. Hours of frustration and a headache later, I had read, followed, and finished the instruction sheet, and I was charged, wired, and ready to go.

> We are not our own, but bought with a price.

The apostle Paul advises us to present our bodies as a living sacrifice, as spiritual worship (see Rom. 12:1) and reminds us that our bodies are the temple of the Holy Spirit. We are not our own, but bought with a price. So, glorify God in your body (see Rom. 6:19–20). I know. I have done that throughout my life. Walking, jogging, hiking, tennis, aerobics with Jane Fonda. Within the last few years, I developed tennis elbow and broke my ankle hiking. May I be finished now? May I have a waiver, please?

The answer is no. I am not dead yet, although some days I feel close. I am still responsible to polish and maintain my temple. A servant of God is called to remain active all his or her days, like Caleb (see Josh. 14:14). I need health and strength. Let me not grow weary, for at the proper time, I will reap the harvest if I do not give up (see 1 Cor. 9:24). I will put my hand to the plow and not look back (see Luke 9:62). Oh, how I want to rejoice with Jesus at the harvest!

So, my Fitbit has become a motivator and accountability partner. Like a personal trainer, it pushes me out of my comfort zone. No mind games, excuses, or fooling the Fitbit; facts are facts, ma'am! But then the Holy Spirit took me to another level, as He often does. This is not just about physical well-being, but my relationship with God.

Choosing Jesus must be a daily, deliberate decision.

"Choose this day whom you will serve (Josh. 24:15). Choosing Jesus must be a daily, deliberate decision. I may choose ten thousand steps each day on my Fitbit, and I may choose the spirit over the flesh. Obedience is my choice. To be obedient is to be observant, compliant, loyal, faithful, devoted to one's call, and under control. That is what I want, Lord.

But Jesus warned us not to become whitened sepulchers filled with dead men's bones. I do not want to look good on the outside but be dead inside (see Matt. 23:27). Just as I predetermine my Fitbit goals, I also set spiritual and eternal goals. Whatever I do is to bring glory to God (see 1 Cor. 10:31). I am intentional. I am resolved, not swayed by emotions and circumstances. It is my will.

> Every challenge requires determination, discipline, direction, and denial.

OK, sometimes the mind is willing, but the flesh is weak. Chocolate, anyone? Ice cream? Perhaps a nap instead of that hike? Not every Fitbit goal is met, and certainly not every spiritual goal. But I press on to obtain the prize (see 1 Cor. 9:24–27, Phil. 3:14). She who is self-indulgent is dead even while she lives (see 1 Tim. 5:6). Ouch!

Every challenge requires determination, discipline, direction, and denial. The gate that leads to life is narrow and the road hard (see Matt. 7:14) Thankfully, He who began a good work in me will be faithful to complete it. I can do all things through Christ, who strengthens me. God will supply every need of mine. To God be the glory for ever and ever (see Phil. 1:6, 4:13, 19–20).

Daniel purposed in his heart not to defile his body and knelt to pray three times each day (see Dan. 1:8, 6:10). Thus, he found favor with God. When I check my Fitbit throughout the day, it is a reminder to pray. When my Fitbit vibrates at the end of the day to tell me I have been successful, I also want Jesus to say, "Today was well done, good and faithful servant." The gate is narrow, and the road is hard, but the reward is eternal. Amen.

Today I will be intentional and resolve to love the Lord my God with my body, mind, and spirit. I will be obedient and compliant, devoted to my high calling as a servant of Christ, taking the narrow road.

CHAPTER 11

God Has My Number
(In Due Time)

S ocial anxiety entered my life uninvited and remained my constant companion for ten years. At times, it was an unsettling undercurrent, but at other times, it was debilitating. Although I had lived an active, satisfying life, anxiety diverted me to a fearful, solitary existence. I left people and projects behind. My days were filled with heaviness and hopelessness. Interaction with people was unbearable. A low-grade dread, sometimes pierced by the pain of panic, was my new normal.

> Anxiety diverted me to a fearful, solitary existence.

This was not the abundant life Jesus promised. We are reminded not to fear people, who can only kill the body but not the soul, but rather fear him who can destroy both body and soul (see Matt. 10:28–33). Satan was a prowling lion seeking to devour me (1 Pet. 5:8). This was a spiritual battle. Wake up, Deborah, wake up! (see Judg. 5:12).

"Even the hairs of your head are numbered. Therefore, fear not" (Matt. 10:30). God has also numbered the days of my life (Ps. 139:16) and numbered every star (Ps. 147:4). He calls the stars by name! Our hair, our days, and the stars are not counted in aggregate numbers, not the total number. God gives a specific, individual number to each one and knows it. "Such knowledge is too wonderful for me; it is high, I cannot attain it (Ps. 139:6). He knows me, He loves me, He cares. He is acquainted with all my ways (see Ps. 139:2). In other words, He's got my number!

I needed serious mending, to be put in working order again. I humbled myself under His mighty hand. Surrendering my mind, will, and emotions, I cast my anxieties upon His loom, and in time, He would lift me up in a new garment (see 1 Pet. 5:6–7). God's Waiting Room was not new to me. I had been there before. Eventually, The Great Physician would see me, heal me, and send me on my way. I was prepared to wait again. But this was to be a very distinctive appointment: ten years in the Waiting Room was not what I had expected.

Ten years in the Waiting Room was not what I had expected.

"For everything there is a season, and a time for every matter under heaven" (Eccles. 3:1). There is a time to weep, laugh, mourn, dance, rend, and sew. The days of each season are numbered and known to God. "One day" and "in the fullness of time" (see 2 Kings 4:8, Gal. 4:4–7) assure me that God is sovereign over all my days. Nothing is lost or forgotten like a misplaced sticky note on His messy desk calendar. Even Jesus said, "My time has not yet come" and "My hour is not yet come" (see John 2:4, 7:6).

"At the set time, which I appoint...," says the Lord God (Ps. 75:2). Indeed, my time to be rewoven and refreshed did arrive. In my affliction, I was bowed down, but I had hope. The steadfastness of the Lord never ceases; His mercies never end. They are new every morning. Great is His faithfulness.

> **If God is for us, what can man do to us?**

The Lord is good to those who wait quietly and seek Him. For the Lord will not cast off forever. Surely, He has my number. He will have compassion. When I cried out, "I am lost," He took up my cause and redeemed my life (Lam. 3:19–59).

Now my goal is to follow the Shepherd one step, one day at a time. I am not anxious to see far in front. He is already there. He begs me to be in the present, in His Presence. Eyes on Jesus, not on people. If God is for us, what can man do to us? This is the peace that passes understanding. This is the day the Lord has made (number 23,705 for me!); I will rejoice and be glad in it!

Today I will wait in quiet confidence, knowing God will lift me up in the fullness of time. I fear no evil, for God is with me. Surely goodness and mercy will follow me all my days.

CHAPTER 12

Take a Nap (Serenity Now!)

Nap time. Every mother with young children awaits those precious hours. I was no different. My days began at 5:30 a.m. Just enough time to shower and dress before my boys got up at 6:00. Gogogogogo. Eat breakfast, sweep underneath the table, load the dishwasher, calm a skirmish, get the boys dressed, brush their teeth, comb their hair, make beds, calm a skirmish, play with Fisher-Price people, read books, play with Hot Wheels, calm a skirmish, ride bikes around the block, wash a load of laundry, fix a snack, clean up after the snack. It was 10:00 a.m.; now what could we do? Go get groceries for a change of scenery. Yay!

Mornings were fun, and loooong. If I could just stay cheerful, energetic, and get through lunch, I was home free. Nap time. Rest and restoration. Renewed enthusiasm and strength to push on until bedtime.

My oldest son was about to outgrow nap time, but his younger brother and his mom still needed the break. I put him in bed, but within minutes he came out, saying, "I can't sleep."

"OK," I said patiently. "Go back to bed and just rest."

He complied but came back again after a short time. "I can't rest," he stated hopefully. No deal.

"Well, then, just go to bed and lie there until I come for you," I replied firmly.

Off he went with no argument. Good. I was finally on the couch, eyes closed, when a little voice whispered gently, "I can't sleep or rest or lie."

Grrrr... Without my nap, I will need chocolate to press on.

When worry and anxiety vex me, I can't sleep or rest or lie. Did God just say "Grrrr?" He has promised that if I am heavy laden, I can go to Him, and He will give me rest. He is gentle, and I will find rest for my soul in Him (see Matt. 11:29–30) But I just will not do it. I come back with a reason or excuse. I need to plan, work, or manipulate until I solve every issue. I have things to do. No nap for me.

God replies firmly, "I tell you, do not be anxious about your life... you of little faith (see Matt. 6: 25, 30). Jesus assures me I can cast all my anxieties on Him because He cares for me (see 1 Pet. 5:7). But I do not need a nap. I can push on in my own strength. After all, I am omnipotent and omniscient, right?

> # Without my nap, I will need chocolate to press on.

Days of painful uneasiness and sleepless nights rob me of peace. This is not the abundant life Jesus came to give me. Worry chokes and strangles; it robs joy and steals hope. The beginning of anxiety is the end of faith. It is atheism.

O my soul, why are you cast down and disquieted within me? Hope in God and praise Him, for He is your help (see Ps. 43:5). Time to take every worrisome, troublesome, doubtful, fearful thought captive to Christ (see 2 Cor. 10:5). Time to replace them with whatsoever is true, just, pure, lovely, and worthy of praise (see Phil. 4:8).

> **Worry chokes and strangles.**

A mother knows what her child needs, and my heavenly Father knows what I need for mental, emotional, physical, and spiritual strength. I can stop getting up, stop arguing. I can lie down and sleep, for the Lord sustains me. In peace, I will both lie down and sleep because He neither slumbers nor sleeps. Unless the Lord watches over the city, the watchman stays awake in vain. God gives His beloveds sleep (see Ps. 3:5, 4:8, 121:4, 127:1–2).

This watchman needs a nap. I will sleep and rest and lie

in the everlasting arms of my eternal God, my refuge (see Deut. 33:27).

Today I will put anxiety, worry, and fear aside as I rest serenely in the peace that Jesus provides. I will cast my burdens on Him, and He will sustain me.

CHAPTER 13

Dragon Lady (Fiery Tongue)

Across the crowded room, at a gathering of friends, I watched an acquaintance arrive. She stopped to scan the group, looking to see who was in attendance, and our eyes met. To my surprise, her gaze stayed locked on me as she made her way through the guests, smiling, and intentionally came to me. After a brief hello and pleasantries, her facial expression changed, and her purpose became clear.

Like a dragon, she opened her mouth of flames and torched me. Hateful, brutal insults and accusations scorched me from head to toe. The surprise attack, the fierceness left me in pained shock until the mercy of numbness set it. I stood speechless as she turned to chitchat and socialize with others. Graciously, Jesus stood with me in that fiery furnace. The Holy Spirit assured me this incineration was without merit. I offered no rebuttal; God would contend for me. I told only my husband.

This was a welder with a blow torch devilishly aimed at me.

James 3 teaches us that the small flame of the tongue can set a forest ablaze. Amen. But this was no small flame. This was a welder with a blow torch devilishly aimed at me. I survived third-degree burns to my soul, but I needed intensive care. Jesus gently covered my wounds with His healing balm and wrapped me tenderly in gauze. However, full recovery would take years. Other issues and circumstances brought infection into my damaged flesh. I needed the Great Physician to attend me. He prescribed an induced coma and literally moved me to a remote location, away from the threat of social encounters.

Dragon Lady (Fiery Tongue)

Our new home and quiet surroundings far out in the desert aided my recuperation. Emotional restoration came by degrees; spiritual rehabilitation had setbacks.

I looked to the Word for healing but found James holding a mirror up to me. I was reminded that we all make mistakes and have difficulty bridling our tongues. Ashamed and painfully aware that I, too, had singed and seared others with my unruly tongue, I asked for forgiveness. Oh, Lord, heal every blister and cover every scar I have caused. Bind up the wounds I have inflicted. Allow my victims to forgive me and rejoice in your faithfulness! Make a garland from their ashes, as only You can (see Isa. 61:3).

> **What another meant for evil, God meant for good.**

Slowly, the charred skin fell off. Revived, I came to realize, as Joseph had, that God is sovereign and had allowed me to be at that event with the Dragon Lady. And, like Joseph, I can say that what another meant for evil, God meant for good (see Gen. 50:20). Although I have forgiven her in my heart, I have also drawn a personal boundary. The wise are to be peaceable, gentle, and full of mercy (see James 3:17). With that in mind, I now wisely keep my distance from the Dragon Lady but respond to her in humility as the occasion arises. I must not bless the Lord yet curse man with the same tongue. "She opens her mouth with wisdom, and the teaching of kindness is on her tongue" (Prov. 31:1). I have far to go...

I have been loved by many and treated well by most. There are hurting, unkind people in the world, and I had just run into one. Such is life. As I enjoy my morning desert walks, it is a pleasure to observe the beauty and variety of God's creation. Sometimes, though, I come upon doggie poop on the sidewalk, allowed and left by a thoughtless pet owner. Really? What kind of person does that? What is wrong with people? How can someone leave that mess and just go on their merry way? Ick! I can let it anger and disturb me. I can think countless ugly thoughts about idiot dog owners. Or I can look away. I can walk a wide path around it, with eyes on nature's glorious display all about me. The choice is mine. I will remember this if I fall into the path of another Dragon Lady—ignore the poop, walk away, and look for the loveliness of others around me.

Dragon Lady (Fiery Tongue)

Today, as I humbly acknowledge that my own tongue has inflicted pain, I look to Jesus to forgive me as I have forgiven others and trust Him to defend me when attacked. I will ignore evil and look for good.

CHAPTER 14

Blind (Inner Beauty)

My annual ob-gyn appointment is an exercise in humility and humiliation. Fortunately, I have known my doctor for thirty years, and he has a fabulous, wry sense of humor. Comic relief was welcome as I sat half-naked before him. After the exam, I pulled out my little note paper with questions I had prepared and did not want to forget. I noticed his smile, pretended to be irritated, and asked, "What?" He answered with a mocking laugh," Well, my more modern patients have their notes on their phones." I was not amused.

A younger friend offered to proofread my first book, Mended: Out of the Rag Pile and Back on the Hanger. I welcomed her help and suggestions wholeheartedly. In one chapter, "White Rabbit," I wrote about the constant tick-tick-ticking in my head telling me, "I'm late. I'm late." The solution had been to get a Day-Timer to write out all goals, responsibilities, events, etc., in a calendar-like book, organizing my life by the hour. My friend returned my manuscript with a note and suggestion on that page. She reminded me that nobody uses a Day-Timer anymore; it was outdated. Perhaps I could rewrite it to say I kept a calendar on my phone or iPad. Like the "more modern" women I had been told about by my doctor? Not amused, but I made the change.

I was out to breakfast with my daughter-in-law and grandchildren. We waited in line to order and, after we finished, she took the kids to find a table. I remained at the counter to get our drinks. As I reached for napkins, one fell to the floor. Without a thought, I bent quickly to retrieve it. That's when I heard the gentleman behind me say, "Well, say, you're still pretty spry."

Spry? Spry, like my ninety-five-year-old mother? Spry, like a white-haired woman with a Dowager's hump and orthopedic shoes? Did he not see my blonde hair, cute shoes, fashionably torn jeans with the cuffs rolled up, and my funky jewelry? Me, spry? What he meant as a compliment pierced me to the core; clearly, I am not the "modern woman" I like to think I am. I was betrayed by my withered, veined hands and crepe-y neck. Oh, and the age spots. And the wrinkles. Although my college roommate knows my true, inner self and assures me I'm still a "fun chick," others don't see me that way. They are not fooled by my smoke and mirrors.

> Spry, like my ninety-five-year-old mother?

Jesus sees the real me, too. While people look at my outward appearance, He sees my heart, patched, and stitched by His gentle hands. Others consider my appearance and height, but God sees not as man sees (see 1 Sam. 16:7). I do well to remember that God treasures those who fear Him and find their hope in His unfailing love (see Ps. 147:11). There is no mention of youth or beauty regarding the Proverbs 31 woman—only her kindness and good deeds. I can only assume she is spry, too. Strength and dignity are her clothing, not fashionable shoes, and earrings. She is not dressed to impress or bring attention to herself. She allows God to shine, not herself. Charm is deceitful and beauty vain, but a woman who fears the Lord shall be praised. Even if she doesn't keep her calendar and notes on an iPad.

Do I offer humor, wisdom, and hope?

I ask myself this: Would a blind person like me? If my outward adornments were unseen, what would others "see" in me? Is my voice warm, friendly, gentle? Are my words kind, encouraging, compassionate? Is my conversation intelligent, relevant, worth hearing? Am I curious and teachable? Do I offer humor, wisdom, and hope? Am I quick to listen and slow to speak? Do people feel better about themselves after spending time with me? Is my conversation worldly, or do I speak of the Kingdom of God? Do my words bring life and peace?

My appearance does not reveal the true me. I may no longer be a modern woman, but I can be an ageless woman of God, bearing good fruit from the abundance of my heart. "The righteous flourish like the palm tree…they still bring forth fruit in old age; they are ever full of sap and green" (Ps. 92:14). God the Father has chosen, appointed, ordained me to bear good fruit, lead a worthy life, and please Him (see John 15:16, Col. 1:10). I will be happy and sow joy, aging gracefully and gratefully. I am a valuable, vintage cloth, woven by the Master Tailor. Beauty is passing, but a woman who fears the Lord shall be praised (see Prov. 31:30).

My appearance does not reveal the true me.

Today I will live in such a way that the blind may see Jesus in me, not depending on my outward appearance, but rather on the fruit of the Spirit.

CHAPTER 15

Overwhelmed (Anxiety)

Just as Jesus intentionally sent His disciples into stormy waters, He allowed the perfect storm of health issues, people, and circumstances to rock my boat. Unplanned early retirement and attacks by the Dragon Lady (mentioned in chapter 13) and others left me stunned and without my lifelong bearings. I was in deep, churning water, and my sails were torn. And as the disciples on the stormy lake cried out, "Lord, do you not care?" (see Mark 4:38), I, too, called to

Jesus. He did know, and He did care, but He had the bigger picture in mind. And He alone would see me safely to the other side ten years later.

Gripped by Social Anxiety Disorder (SAD, ironically), I canceled everything, including the precious Bible study I led. I saw almost no one. This profound anxiety can be defined as a painful, abnormal apprehension; uneasiness of mind and a self-doubt about one's ability to cope. Getting groceries was a nightmare. Answering the phone gave me heart palpitations. I could no longer go to church. E-mails from friends went unanswered, and invitations to events became "regrets." Attempts to self-medicate with vast quantities of chocolate left me fat, and still anxious. Great. I became Jabba the Hut, with no clothing that would fit. Depression, added to anxiety, calls for one thing: more chocolate, right? Oh, and maybe a glass of wine.

> ## Invitations to events became "regrets."

"When my spirit overwhelmed me, you knew my path" (see Ps. 142:3). In Hebrew, "overwhelmed" means to be covered with a garment; to be covered as with darkness, sorrow; to be faint, feeble. It holds the idea of "the muffling of my spirit"; to be smothered, confused, distracted, unable to choose, wrapped in thick gloom. I was, indeed, overwhelmed! What was this new wardrobe? I did not choose to wear these items! I sat at home, wrapped in a thick, heavy garment of darkness, with a muffler of sorrow smothering and strangling me. I was clothed in fear, suffocating to death.

I was clothed in fear, suffocating to death.

But Jesus knew my path. No trouble or danger is concealed from Him. When a heavy fog settled on my mind, His eternal Mind was clear. When I moaned, and was so troubled I could not speak, He was gracious. He led me (see Psalm 77). When my soul fainted, He delivered me (see Psalm 107). He removed the heavy garment of trouble and replaced it with a robe of peace.

Over time, I learned to cast my anxiety on Him. He asks me to do so; He gives me permission; He cares for me (see 1 Peter 5:6–7). In Greek, "to cast" means to make someone else responsible; to put the responsibility on another. Jesus is responsible for me. What freedom! In my weakness, His power is perfected. "Anxiety in a man's heart weighs him down" (Prov. 12:25) like a heavy chain. This is a heaviness we are not designed to wear.

I needed to learn to give up fear for trust. Fear distracts the mind and causes a loss of perspective. "Have no anxiety about anything..." Constant prayer and thanksgiving are the remedy. Peace beyond our understanding follows (see Phil. 4:6–7). Peace—in Hebrew, "shalom"—means wholeness and well-being. Only Jesus could make my tattered, frayed soul whole and fill me with a sense of well-being, replacing apprehension, heaviness, and gloom. I could not force myself to be peaceful, but as I gratefully acknowledged God's past mercies and focused on His generosity, He gave me His spirit of tranquility.

> # Jesus is responsible for me. What freedom!

It was a slow process. At times, people or circumstances draped me again in that heavy garment of mental darkness. Sometimes, I picked up the muffler of despair and wrapped my own neck with it. But the longer I sat in His presence, the easier it was to cast off that suffocating apparel. "Peace I leave you; my peace I give to you. Not as the world gives do I give to you. Let not your hearts be troubled; neither let them be afraid" (John 14:27). The world offers chocolate and wine, but they are not the solution. Jesus, only Jesus.

I press on with the peace of God guarding my heart and mind in Jesus Christ (see Phil. 4:7). The Holy Spirit is a soldier standing within the gate to prevent an invasion of fear. As I continue to think on whatever is true, honorable, just, pure, lovely, noble, excellent, and worthy of praise, the peace of God is with me. I have learned to be content in all circumstances (well, most of the time) and allow Him to strengthen me (see Phil. 4:8–13).

Today I will empty my hands of the sharp rocks of fear and anxiety, turning my helpless palms up in praise and gratitude as I trust Jesus for the peace that surpasses understanding.

PART 2

"Little" Alterations

CHAPTER 16

The "Littles" (Trust)

Unexpectedly, I became involved in the lives of three young boys more than twelve years ago. Big brother was just twenty months old when his twin brothers arrived. Yes, three boys under the age of two! In addition, the eldest had autism, and the twins had craniosynostosis. I had no grandchildren yet, so they were a gift from heaven. I was at their home daily for six months. After that, I visited several times each week. Despite the challenges, multiple surgeries, and therapies, each child was a delight with unique talents, gifts, and personalities. My regular involvement continues to this day. God had countless lessons in store for me. As I watched them develop, I saw parallels in my own spiritual growth.

> God had countless lessons in store for me.

Older brother Cole could not pronounce the babies' names, Colin and Conor, so he called them "Con-Con." Adorable. We also called them The Babies, The Twins, Pete and Repeat, Thing One and Thing Two, The Bubbas, The Monkeys, our Joy Boys. As they grew, we needed to distinguish between the brothers or the boys. The Mommy began to say, "the Little Boys" or "the Little Brothers," which eventually became just "The Littles." Perfect.

My husband and I regularly took The Littles out on adventures. They were delightful company, it broadened their life experience, and it gave the Mommy a much-needed break. We went anywhere and everywhere together to see and do things: parks, splash pads, malls, the pet store, the balloon man, restaurants, our house, my husband's office, resort hotels, museums, Frontier Town, zoos, aquariums, the bookstore, toy stores, the golf course, the pool, Christmas displays, neighborhood walks, bike rides, duck ponds, the rodeo, our cabin in the pines, sledding. As we drove to our destinations, we sang songs, made up stories, told jokes, teased, and laughed. Never a dull moment, and never a bad time.

Eventually, trust and innocence faded.

Eventually, trust and innocence faded. They lost their childlike faith in us and had their own ideas. As I eagerly told The Littles the plan for the day, they appeared less than enthusiastic. They had questions. We debated. I defended my fun activity. Then I heard it: "But we want to do what we want to do!" What? After all these years of love and wonderful adventures and memories together, you can't trust me? Just get in the car!

Hmmm...this sounded familiar. The Littles argued with me, just as I argue with God. Not good. Foolishness, really. Who knows best? Who has more information, more insight? Who sees the bigger picture? Who is wiser? Who should make the plan, and who should shut up and follow? And what about the trust earned from past faithfulness? What changed? Don't those years and experiences prove anything?

I am a misguided, stubborn, strong-willed, opinionated Little. Sometimes, I relax and happily let Jesus make the plan and lead the way. Other times, I want to do what I want to do! Listen as Jesus gently rebukes me: "Where were you when I laid the foundation of the Earth? Tell me, if you have understanding…have you commanded the morning since your days began? Where is the way to the dwelling of the light? Declare, if you know…is it by your wisdom that the hawk soars? He who argues with God, let him answer…will you put me in the wrong that you may be justified?" (see Job 38–40) Oh, Lord, forgive my arrogance. "I have uttered what I did not understand, things too wonderful for me, which I did not know (Job 42:3).

> I want to live daily with the faith of a child.

OK, Lord, put me back on the loom and refashion my thinking. I want to live daily with the faith of a child. "No good thing does the Lord withhold from those who walk uprightly…

blessed is the man who trusts in thee (Ps. 84:11–12). "Those who seek the Lord lack no good thing" (Ps. 34:10). The grace of God is His goodwill toward men. Infinite wisdom provides all good things in due time and protects me from what is not good. And so it is with The Littles. They will lack no good thing if they will just trust me. They can have peace and freedom and joy knowing that I will faithfully and lovingly plan good things and lead them on a good path. Just get in the car!

"No eye has seen, nor ear heard, nor the heart conceived what God has prepared (planned) for those who love him" (1 Cor. 2:9). The Lord is my Shepherd. He calls me by name and leads me in the way I should go. I know His voice and follow Him. He leads me beside still water for rest and healing. He leads me through the valley of death with His guidance and protection. He lays down His life for me (see Psalm 23 and John 10). I just need to get in the car.

Today I will set aside my own plans and be content to trust Jesus, wherever He leads me. His thoughts and His ways are higher than mine.

CHAPTER 17

Running Legs (Rebellion)

In the past ten years, I have spent thousands of hours in the company of "The Littles." My vocabulary is too limited to describe them, but the short list would include creative, imaginative, inquisitive, curious, bright, and hyperactive. An active mind and an active body is a dangerous combination in young boys!

Their living arrangements constrained them to one small

living room. They were gated off from the kitchen (dangerous) and the dog (for his peace and safety), as well as the upstairs bedrooms. Attempts were made to keep them active: a ball pit, a minitrampoline, a small slide, and a crawling tunnel crowded the room. Daily, they jumped on the couch or turned it into a fort, as any boys would. They were playful and content, but any opportunity to go outdoors was welcome. My husband's car became an amusement park as they raised and lowered windows, turned on the windshield wipers, honked the horn, flashed the turn signal, and poked their heads out the sunroof while moving the seats forward and back. Radio on, headlights on—joy! New outside adventures offered exercise and education as they burned energy and built vocabulary and life experience.

Paradise for visiting adults and certainly heaven for The Littles.

My husband and I loved to take them to a nearby resort hotel. The grounds were beautifully manicured with flowers and fountains. After a quick joy ride on the fancy gold luggage carts, The Littles entered the wide-open five-story courtyard lobby, with a fountain that cascaded down over two stories. Just outside the lobby was a large patio area overlooking a small grass island surrounded by a water feature with ducks. Paradise for visiting adults and certainly heaven for The Littles.

On one occasion, as we arrived at the massive parking lot, I began to review the rules. For their safety and good manners, I reminded the boys that this was a public area with adult guests, not a playground. No running, climbing, jumping, or loud voices were allowed. They were to hold our hands and remain with us. They listened intently, and one replied candidly, "Well, you're gonna have to carry me, 'cuz I have running legs!"

> ## Lord, you're gonna have to carry me 'cuz I just won't obey!

We burst out laughing at his accurate appraisal of the situation, but he seemed surprised at our response. He wasn't being funny, just honest—wanting to obey, but knowing his own nature.

Sweet Jesus, how often is this my cry, too? Lord, you're

gonna have to carry me 'cuz I just won't obey! An old hymn echoes this lament: "Let thy goodness, like a fetter, bind my wandering heart to thee. Prone to wander; Lord, I feel it, prone to leave the God I love." Amen, amen. No matter what gracious, lovely life adventure He has planned just for me, I may "run ahead" and ruin it with my headstrong, rebellious ways. I need to confess it, admit it, and plead with God to thwart my misbehavior. Carry me, Jesus.

I know the rules; I need no reminders. I have been here before. So many things inside me are still difficult to overcome and control. I need to surrender. I need to walk by the Spirit, not the flesh (see Gal. 5:16–17). No more good intentions. Only the Spirit will bear the fruit of self-control in me (see Gal. 5:22). Trusting Jesus rather than self is

Obedience is a choice.

the answer, the only way. This requires alterations only the Holy Spirit can make.

The dictionary definition of **obedience** includes compliance, submission, loyalty, homage, and devotion. Choose each day whom you shall serve (see Josh. 24:15). Obedience is a choice. Those who choose another god multiply their sorrow (Ps. 16:4). How well I know this. Whenever I choose another god, the result is ugly, sometimes painful. I find myself living with my own seven dwarfs: Grumpy, Selfish, Angry, Impatient, Arrogant, Self-Righteous, and Thankless. Wake up, Deborah! Wake up! (Judg. 5:12) This is a spiritual battle. If today you hear His voice, harden not your heart (Ps. 95:8). Each day, Jesus calls to me, yearns for my fellowship and loyalty. He has a big day at the resort planned for me. If I let Him carry me, I won't miss out. I may even get to ride on the luggage cart! But if I have running legs, disaster looms.

That day we successfully arrived at the grass island without incident. Suddenly, the other brother dropped my hand and sped across the grass toward a large blanket on the ground with balloons tethered to gifts. Someone had briefly abandoned their party area. When I caught up, I reminded him of the hand-holding rule: "Do not run ahead; it is not safe!"

With gleeful innocence, eyes bright, and a wide smile, he exclaimed, "There might be cake!"

I had to laugh as I recognized the universal cry of all sinners: "I let go of your hand, Lord, and break the rules 'cuz

I want cake!"

I have learned much from the Littles. When I was a child, I spoke, thought, and acted as a child; but now I have grown and put away childish things (see 1 Corinthians 11–12) As I surrender my will to the will of the Father, emotions or circumstances no longer drive me. Childish mind games, justifications, rationalizations, and excuses are set aside. I will not allow my running legs to determine my path. I will not be a wild child. I will allow the Holy Spirit to fill and guide me. You're gonna have to carry me, Jesus.

> I will not be a wild child.

Today, as I confess my tendency to leave Jesus, I will ask Him, with the faith of a child, to carry me for my own safety and good

.

CHAPTER 18

On Your Bottom (Yielding)

After an endlessly active morning and the trials of lunch with twin toddlers, it was finally, blessedly time for naps. The Littles raced each other to the top of the stairs, pushing, pulling, and laughing on each step. Lord, give me strength. In fifteen minutes, I would have a break.

In their bedroom, they each searched for a book for me to read before putting them to bed. In the hunt, they threw ten other books onto the floor as they found their favorites somewhere near the bottom of the basket. They selected **Brown Brown Bear** and *The Very Hungry Caterpillar.* Again.

OK, now the transition from lively to calm. Close the curtains and dim the light. Time to sit with no wiggling, jumping, squirming, rolling, poking, talking, or silliness. They know the drill. They know me. Nothing new. We sit in our little reading circle quietly. "On your bottom."

Soulful pleading and apologies followed.

One Little followed instructions. The other one, however, stood. "On your bottom," I reminded him softly. He smiled and jumped. "No, on your bottom so we can read," I said more sternly. Still smiling, he squatted halfway down. "That is not sitting," I warned. He lowered himself, but still not "on your bottom."

I stood up, put the books back in the basket, and began to put them in bed without story time. The desperate crying and wailing was so loud, the neighbors could hear it, I am sure. Soulful pleading and apologies followed. Without a word, I placed each in his crib and left the room. Lesson learned?

On Your Bottom (Yielding)

The next day, at naptime, the Littles flew up the stairs, found their books, and were seated before I entered the room. "Look," one of them said, smiling. "We are on our bottoms!"

Lesson learned!

Again, I see myself in them. Obedience means compliance, restraint, under control, submission, faithfulness, devotion. It is choosing to yield. Ouch. I, too, know the drill. I have learned the right way from wrong (see Ps. 119:1–16). The Word of God instructs me in the way I should go. The Holy Spirit prompts and reminds me. Yet at times I will not yield. Squatting halfway, I smile at God to see if it is enough. Can I get away with just a little disobedience without consequences?

> Like Eve in the garden, I sometimes listen to Satan's lies.

The Mommy teaches deaf children. I also shared a classroom with a sign language teacher when I taught Spanish. I have come to appreciate the signs and movements that express the thoughts of the deaf. The concepts of obedience and obey are shown by both hands close to the forehead with palms inward, then brought forward, with palms facing up. It suggests a mind offering to cooperate. Beautiful.

When I refuse to cooperate with Jesus, my sinful nature tells me God won't mind a little compromise. A bit of gossip or impatience, a critical thought or judgment, an evening of overeating won't hurt. I am too foolish to think about how my rebellious action will affect me, or others, or my future. Is this a wise decision? Is the pleasure worth the pain? Like Eve in the garden, I sometimes listen to Satan's lies. God has given me truth, His Word, for my good, my protection, but at times I do not want to hear it. The result can be painful, and others pay the price for my disobedience, too. Sin splatters. Like the Littles, I wail and gnash my teeth, to no avail. Lesson learned.

Again, I must choose to stay "on my bottom," on bended knee, bowed down. "Let us kneel before the Lord our Maker...if today you hear His voice, harden not your heart" (see Ps. 95:6–8). I must choose a mental posture of humility, submission, and worship. Your Word is my delight. Let my soul live, and I shall praise You, Lord.

Today I will yield my thoughts, my mind, to cooperate with Jesus, allowing the Holy Spirit to direct my choices and my actions.

CHAPTER 19

Blah, Blah, Blah (God's Word)

The Littles do not live close to us. A round trip from our house to theirs can take an hour. If we add an adventure or another destination, it is a lo-o-ong time together in the car. For eager, excited, inquisitive, hyperactive boys, it could be the best of times or the worst of times. I always came prepared. Jokes, riddles, I Spy, fun Q & A games, songs, alphabet games. When I ran out of ideas, we looked at cloud formations to find animal shapes and other items from their imagination. On cloudless days, we resorted to looking at the saguaro cacti, with varying heights and arms, to entertain us. We gave them names, personalities, occupations, activities, and conversations that occurred among them.

On many occasions, the twins provided their own fun by making up stories. I was relieved of the pressure to entertain them. One ongoing saga from trip to trip involved Dr. Gorilla and his assistant, Squid. They took turns but always seemed to go in the same story direction, as if they were of one mind. It was fascinating to hear. One would describe Dr. Gorilla in detail and begin the plot line. The other would pick up with Squid, again with meticulous description, and advance the tale. Always elaborate and hysterical, the narrative never ended. "To be continued..."

We resorted to looking at the saguaro cacti.

Once, as I was attempting to amuse and distract them, one Little finally expressed his disinterest: "Blah blah blah!" We all burst into laughter. Point made. Drive faster or come up with something else. After so many hours and miles together, they had high expectations. Change up the routine.

Turn on the radio, or put in a CD—anything.

That was not the end, however. Within a few weeks, I was surprised and delighted to find a large, black wooden sign with white capital letters. "Blah Blah Blah" was written, one word stacked atop the other. I chuckled, bought it immediately, and placed it in a prominent location in the family room. It became a mantra for my husband and me. Even later, at a craft store, I found a stamp with "Blah Blah Blah" on it. So many opportunities to use that little gem.

> One Little finally expressed his disinterest: "Blah blah blah!"

Finally, the day came when the Littles were coming to our house again. After yet another long drive, we arrived, and I ushered them to the family room. I was exploding with anticipation of the fun and laughter ahead. Instead, the same Little, with a twinkle in his eye and an irresistible smile, declared, "Blah blah blah with your blah blah blah sign. What is something fun we can do?"

My husband and I split our seams with laughter.

Another little alteration was made in my spirit. I realized that I say, "Blah blah blah" in my heart at times. Maybe the Sunday sermon is too long or not a topic of interest to me. Sometimes my devotional book is about a Bible verse I have read many times. It might be a Bible study theme I have already learned. Blah blah blah. Nothing new here, nothing to learn, no claps of thunder or angels singing on high. I want to be entertained. What else ya got?

It continues subtly each day. We have hung various crosses and Scriptures around our home. Not as a sign of our holiness, but rather a reminder to us that we are saved by grace. Therefore, we are to grow and show the fruit of the Spirit daily (see Gal. 5:22 and John 15:4). I must abide in Jesus, being alert to His presence. I easily and frequently pass by our decor without a thought or acknowledgment of their meaning. Blah blah blah with your Word of God. What is something fun I can do?

> How can I ever feel blah about His Word?

Blah, Blah, Blah (God's Word)

"Thou hast exalted above everything thy name and thy word" (Ps. 138:2). God's Word revives the soul, makes the simple wise, rejoices the heart, enlightens, and warns, and is to be desired more than gold (see Ps. 19:7–11). What a gift He has given us! How can I ever feel blah about His Word? Forgive me, Jesus.

Paul instructs Timothy to preach the sacred writings urgently. All Scripture is inspired by God and profitable for teaching (what is right), reproof (what is not right), correction (how to get right), and training (how to stay right). He warns that the time is coming that people will not endure sound teaching but will turn away from truth to suit their own liking (see 2 Tim. 3:14–4:4). In other words, they will say, "Blah blah blah" to God and His Word of truth and life. Clearly, we are living in that time.

Now our big "blah" sign, although not spiritual decor, serves a higher purpose. It not only gives me a smile when I remember my dear Littles; it also serves as a heart check.

I want to live in the Spirit throughout my daily routine, my mundane life, not longing for bells and whistles or constant amusement. Life is never blah with Jesus, and certainly not with the Littles.

Today I will serve the Lord with gladness and come into His presence with singing, rather than turning to things of my own liking for excitement and entertainment.

CHAPTER 20

Mommy Love
(God's Limitless Love)

The Littles are irresistible. Really. I just want to eat them, tickle them, and zubber their tummies (make "raspberries"). There is something mystical, magical, fascinating about twins. I need self-restraint to avoid being questioned by Child Protective Services! My love is harmless, innocent, pure, and overwhelming, yet it must be contained.

Lord, help me.

My only recourse is to tell them constantly, "I love you." I love, love, love, love you. You make my heart happy. You make my heart explode. You are my happy place. I'm so glad God gave you to me. You are so wonderful that God made two of you. I love you more than ice cream. More than chocolate. Then I kiss them on their heads a minimum of twenty times per visit. Obsession is putting it mildly.

I found humongous agape love in Jesus.

I have tried in vain to explain and quantify the enormity of my love to them. To the moon and back, to heaven, bigger than the universe. Not even close. One day, I told the Littles I had humongous love for them. Focused and trying to comprehend what I said, one asked for clarification. "Is that more than Mommy love?" Oh, my heart. They had known and experienced the greatest of human love—the sacrificing, unending, unconditional love of Mommy. What could be greater? I quickly assured them that Mommy love is the ultimate love, and humongous love is just a little less than that.

I missed any kind of Mommy love, but I found humongous agape love in Jesus. Unearned, unconditional, unending, unknowable. Just as I tried to explain my love to the twins, words and definitions are inadequate. How does my simple mind comprehend a love that is gentle, yet furious; tender, yet relentless? Eternal, steadfast, everlasting. Personalized and specific to only me, yet available to everyone.

For a child to know and rest assured in Mommy love, it must be experienced. And so it is with God's love. Scholars and philosophers may research and study the subject yet never personally and profoundly know it. Only as Jesus revealed Himself to me could I comprehend that He so loved the world, and me, that He came to die in my place (see John 3:16). While I was lost and dead in sin, He died for me (see Rom. 5:8). For as high as the heavens are above the Earth, so great is His love for me (see Ps .103:11). There is no greater love than to lay down one's life for another (see John 15:13). The Mommy would do this for The Littles. Indeed, she does it daily and would make the ultimate sacrifice without hesitation. I know her.

God is love (1 John 4:16). It is His nature; He can be nothing else. When I learned this overwhelming truth, every tear and rip of my soul began to mend. There is no fear in love. Like a child leaping into his father's awaiting arms, I can take that leap of faith with the assurance that my heavenly Father is there to catch me, always. Jesus came to give me an abundant life, not one of rags and tatters. He patched what others had slit and cut, what circumstances had worn and frayed. The Master Tailor salvaged my rags and redesigned my life for His glory. "How wonderful; how marvelous, is my Savior's love for me," as the old hymn reminds me.

There is no fear in love.

For fifty years, nothing has separated me from the love of God (see Rom. 8:35–39). Not tribulation or peril, not man or principalities, not a teen pregnancy or a drunk driver, not PMS or menopause, not social anxiety disorder. Not even my own stubborn, rebellious, flawed, weak, inconsistent, unsteady self. Hourly, daily, God actively manifests His unstoppable love for me, His raggedy child. It is more than humongous.

Today I will jump into Abba Father's arms as He sings over me and holds me securely in

His arms of grace, forgiveness, and love, kissing me repeatedly on my head.

About the Author

Debbie Woods identifies with Gideon as "the least in my clan." And like Amos, she says, "I am a nobody, but the Lord took me up", with no training, aspiration for greatness or leadership, and showed me favor. Damaged by life, and saved by grace, Debbie was salvaged and rewoven by Jesus. His loving redesign allowed a high school drop-out to become a Spanish teacher who traveled and lived abroad. During her teaching career, she led and assisted high school students on Mexico Mission ministries and European study trips. She supervised over fifty students annually in her Spanish Club activities, and was honored to be named five times to Who's Who Among American Teachers.

Debbie's heart cries out like King David: "Who am I that you have done this for me? But it was a small thing in your sight. .. according to your own heart, to make your servant know it" (see 2 Sam. 7:18). As Elizabeth questioned, "Why am I so favored?", Debbie proclaims, "The Lord has dealt bountifully with me."

In retirement, Debbie became 'The CraPft Queen", creating altered items that she says are "more crap than craft." Her focus is on blessing others, not artistic perfection. She and her husband, Tom, have three sons and four grandchildren.

IF YOU'RE A FAN OF THIS BOOK, PLEASE TELL OTHERS

- [ ] Write about it on your blog and on Twitter and on your Facebook and LinkedIn pages.

- [ ] Suggest it to friends.

- [ ] When you're in a bookstore, ask them if they carry the book. The book is available through all major distributors, so any bookstore that does not have it can easily order it.

- [ ] Write a positive review on www.amazon.com.

- [ ] Send my publisher, HigherLife Publishing (media@ahigherlife.com), suggestions about websites, conferences, and events you know of where this book could be offered.

- [ ] Purchase additional copies to give away as gifts.

❑ You may contact the author at Mendeddebbie2016@gmail.com.

❑ Follow Debbie's blog on Facebook at On the Mend with Debbie.

❑ Both books, Mended: Out of the Rag Pile, Back on the Hanger and Tailored: Being Fitted to Perfection, are available at Amazon. com/author/debbiewoods.